Dying
OCEANS

BY PAULA HOGAN

ENVIRONMENT ALERT!

Gareth Stevens Children's Books
MILWAUKEE

For a free color catalog describing Gareth Stevens' list of high-quality children's books, call 1-800-341-3569 (USA) or 1-800-461-9120 (Canada).

Library of Congress Cataloging-in-Publication Data

Hogan, Paula Z.
    Dying oceans / Paula Hogan.
        p. cm.
    Summary: Discusses the ecological balance of life in the world's oceans and how it is endangered by ocean pollution.
    ISBN 0-8368-0476-7
    1. Marine pollution—Environmental aspects—Juvenile literature. 2. Marine ecology—Juvenile literature. [1. Marine pollution. 2. Marine ecology. 3. Pollution. 4. Ecology. 5. Conservation of natural resources.] I. Title.
QH545.W3H64 1991
363.73'94'09162—dc20   91-10216

A Gareth Stevens Children's Books edition

Edited, designed, and produced by
Gareth Stevens Children's Books
1555 North RiverCenter Drive, Suite 201
Milwaukee, Wisconsin 53212, USA

Picture Credits
AP/ Wide World Photos, front cover (inset); © Tom Bean/DRK Photo, p. 9 (lower); © Jett Britnell/DRK Photo, p. 9 (upper); © Coffey/Greenpeace, pp. 24-25; © Dorreboom/Greenpeace, p. 18 (upper) , 23 (lower); © Jeff Foott/DRK Photo, p. 10 (upper); Ted H. Funk/Third Coast, © 1988, pp. 2-3; © Grace/Greenpeace, pp. 24-25 (inset); © Greenpeace, p. 24; Grant Heilman, Grant Heilman Photography, pp. 20-21; © Stephen J. Krasemann/DRK Photo, pp. 4, 17; © Andrew J. Martinez, The National Audubon Society Collection/ Photo Researchers, Inc., covers, p. 27; © Midgley/Greenpeace, pp. 10-11, 19; Mark Mille/DeWalt & Associates, pp. 6-7 (both), 13, 14-15; © Morgan/ Greenpeace, pp. 12-13, 22; © J.W. Mowbray, The National Audubon Society Collection/ Photo Researchers, Inc., p. 26; NASA, p. 5; Pat Ortega, pp. 8, 16; © Ott/ Greenpeace, p. 23 (upper); © Ron Romanosky/Greenpeace, p. 11; © Don & Pat Valenti/DRK Photo, p. 18 (lower); © Gary R. Zahm/DRK Photo, p. 15.

Series editors: Kelli Peduzzi and Patricia Lantier-Sampon
Series designer: Laurie Shock
Book designer: Sabine Huschke
Picture researchers: Daniel Helminak and Diane Laska
Research editor: Jamie Daniel
Editorial Assistant: Scott Enk

Printed in the United States of America

2 3 4 5 6 7 8 9 9 97 96 95 94 93

At this time, Gareth Stevens, Inc., does not use 100 percent recycled paper, although the paper used in our books does contain about 30 percent recycled fiber. This decision was made after a careful study of current recycling procedures revealed their dubious environmental benefits. We will continue to explore recycling options.

Production Director   President

CONTENTS

Words that appear in the glossary are printed in **boldface** type the first time they appear in the text.

THE SEA AROUND US

The Watery Planet

Earth is a watery planet. Over 70 percent of its surface is covered by large bodies of salt water called **oceans**. The waters of the ocean churn with **currents**, waves, and **tides**. The oceans teem with life. Thousands of kinds of sea creatures live in the salty depths. Oceans give us much of our **oxygen** and food. They keep our planet cool. Without oceans, much of life on Earth could not survive.

The oceans are so big that once we thought nothing could harm them. Today we know this isn't true. They have become a

Below: After laying its eggs in the sand, a sea turtle returns to the ocean in Playa Naranjo, Costa Rica.

poisonous stew of garbage, chemicals, and **sewage** that threatens our health. These **pollutants** kill fish and marine **mammals**. Also, many **species** are being fished and hunted to **extinction**. The oceans are more fragile than anyone ever imagined. If we don't treat them with greater care, sea life will disappear. Millions of humans who depend on the sea for their food and livelihoods will suffer.

Above: Earth has more water than other planets in our solar system. This is because the Earth's temperature usually stays between 32°F (0°C), the freezing point of water, and 212°F (100°C), the boiling point. Other planets are either too warm or too cold to have oceans.

Right: The sea contains 330 million cubic miles (1.37 billion cu km) of water! Dry land covers less than 29 percent of the Earth's surface.

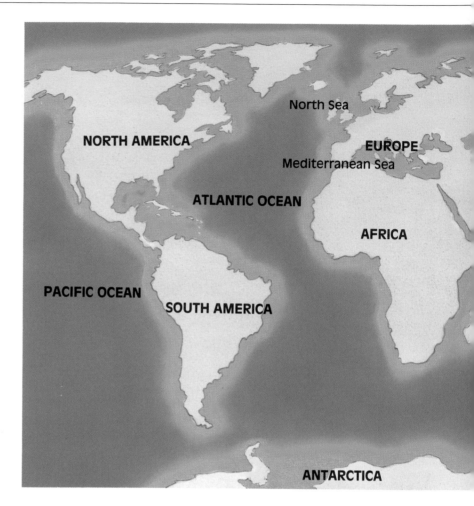

North Sea

NORTH AMERICA

EUROPE

Mediterranean Sea

ATLANTIC OCEAN

AFRICA

PACIFIC OCEAN

SOUTH AMERICA

ANTARCTICA

volcanic island

trench

Oceans of the World

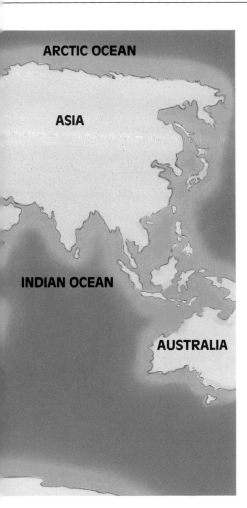

The continental shelf is part of the seafloor that skirts the edge of most large land-masses. The shelf is shallow enough for sunlight to reach the ocean bottom. Thus, it is the only place where plants can grow on the seafloor. Most marine animals also live on the shelf, where food is so plentiful. In some ways, this is a tragedy because the continental shelf is so close to land that it is the most polluted part of the ocean.

Below: The ocean bottom isn't perfectly flat. The continental shelf borders most large land-masses, and mountain ranges and deep trenches stretch for thousands of miles along the ocean floor. The deepest point is in the Pacific Ocean, where the Mariana Trench descends 35,840 feet (10,924 m) below the seafloor.

continental shelf

ocean floor

Surviving the Open Sea

Most ocean dwellers are fish. Air-breathing mammals, such as dolphins, whales, and seals, also live in the ocean. These creatures are strong enough to swim through the ocean's tides and currents. Their stream-lined shapes permit them to move swiftly through water.

In addition to speed, coloring protects fish. Because there is almost nowhere to hide in the open sea, most fish are green or blue, the color of the water. Almost all fish stay near the surface, just below their main food sources, **plankton** and **copepods**.

Only a few kinds of animal plankton and the fish that feed on them live in the deepest, darkest part of the ocean. Here, plants can't grow, so food and shelter are scarce. Bottom-dwelling fish are not strong swimmers, but they have other ways of surviving. The viper fish, for example, has a huge set of teeth.

Above: The Pacific octopus lives on the deep, dark ocean floor.

Opposite: Most fish, such as sunfish (1) and marlin (2), live near the ocean's surface. Ocean plants and animals, such as kelp (3) and coral (4), also live close to the top, where they get plenty of sunlight. Farther down in the middle depths lurk sharks (5), sea horses (6), starfish (7), giant squid (8), and whales. In the sunless depths live strange-looking creatures, such as lantern fish (9), viper fish (10), shrimp (11), and snipe eels (12), whose bodies make their own light to help them see.

Right: At least 4,000 different kinds of seaweed grow in the ocean. Kelp, one of the largest marine plants, has no roots but clings to rocks on the bottom.

9

The Poisoned Seas

We depend on the oceans for our very lives. Without oceans, Earth would be too hot and there would not be enough air to breathe. Yet we treat oceans like open garbage dumps. Because of this, the oceans are in danger of dying. Millions of people who earn a living from the sea are losing their jobs. The fishing industry has been hurt because tons of fish die from pollution. Tourists stay away from many seaside areas because the beaches are polluted with sewage, medical wastes, and garbage. People who make their living working for the tourists earn less. Whales and many kinds of fish are being hunted to extinction.

If we do not try to save the oceans from destruction, much of the life in the sea will die. Without the oceans to balance the climate of our planet and provide us with food, jobs, and recreation, our own lives will be in danger. In some areas, we can already see the cost of neglecting the oceans. We must act to save them before it is too late.

The Vanishing Whale

For centuries, whales have been hunted for meat and oil. Today, every type of whale is endangered. The International Whaling Commission has called for a stop to all whale hunting. Many nations have stopped. But other nations, such as Japan and Iceland, still hunt whales.

Garbage dumped into the oceans washes up on the shore. This garbage not only looks disgusting, but may carry diseases.

Right: Tanker ships spill three to six million tons of oil into the sea each year. These spills are very expensive and difficult to clean up.

FACT FILE
The Mediterranean Sea, the Most Polluted in the World

The Mediterranean Sea is the most polluted in the world! Tons of **pesticides** and other **toxic** chemicals are dumped into it. These pollutants build up year after year. They darken the water and cover life on the seafloor with a deadly ooze.

Factories and ships dump over 300,000 tons of oil into the Mediterranean each year. People who eat Mediterranean seafood also eat the oil these creatures have absorbed. Many Mediterranean cities dump raw sewage along their beachfronts. Raw sewage can cause sickness or even death to swimmers. It also lowers the oxygen level in water so fish can't breathe.

In 1975, all but one of the Mediterranean nations decided to clean up the sea. They agreed to control pollution and set up rules against dumping oil. Large Mediterranean cities, such as Naples, Italy, and Athens, Greece, promised to build sewage treatment plants. Many factories have stopped dumping most toxic wastes into the sea.

Since 1975, Mediterranean pollution has held steady, but it is still bad. Cleanup is so costly that many Mediterranean countries may be too poor to afford it.

Opposite: The Mediterranean Sea is bordered by fifteen nations, two island states, one principality (Monaco), and one colony (Gibraltar). One hundred and twenty cities pollute its waters.

Below: The Europa Point Dump in Gibraltar, on the southern tip of Spain, receives 45 tons of garbage daily. Much of this ends up in the sea.

12

LOWERING THE TOXIC TIDE

Reducing Chemicals

Many factories pour out deadly chemical wastes every day. Some are dumped directly into the sea. Others are poured into rivers that eventually flow into the oceans. As a result of toxic dumping, marine life has almost disappeared from the White Sea off the northwestern coast of the Soviet Union. Fewer and fewer fish are caught in the North Sea. And the Mediterranean Sea is in terrible shape.

Below: Ocean pollution comes from many sources. For example, some factories (1) are heavy polluters. But it is often difficult to prove exactly which industries are at fault. Crop dusters (2), nuclear power plants (3), and rigs that are set up to drill for oil underwater (4) release toxic substances that pollute our oceans. Sometimes, huge ships carrying oil or lethal chemicals (5) have spills that spread over huge areas of the ocean. Toxic garbage (6) often ends up on the seafloor.

Many countries are working through the United Nations' Regional Seas Program to hold down pollution. In Germany, the government made factory owners pay heavy fines for dumping tons of toxic wastes into the Ruhr River. The polluters decided that cleaning up the river was cheaper than paying the fine. Today, the Ruhr is one of the cleanest rivers in Europe.

In the U.S., the state of Washington has put some company presidents in jail for breaking pollution laws. Oil companies also must pay when their tanker ships spill oil into the sea.

These gizzard shad died from swimming in polluted waters.

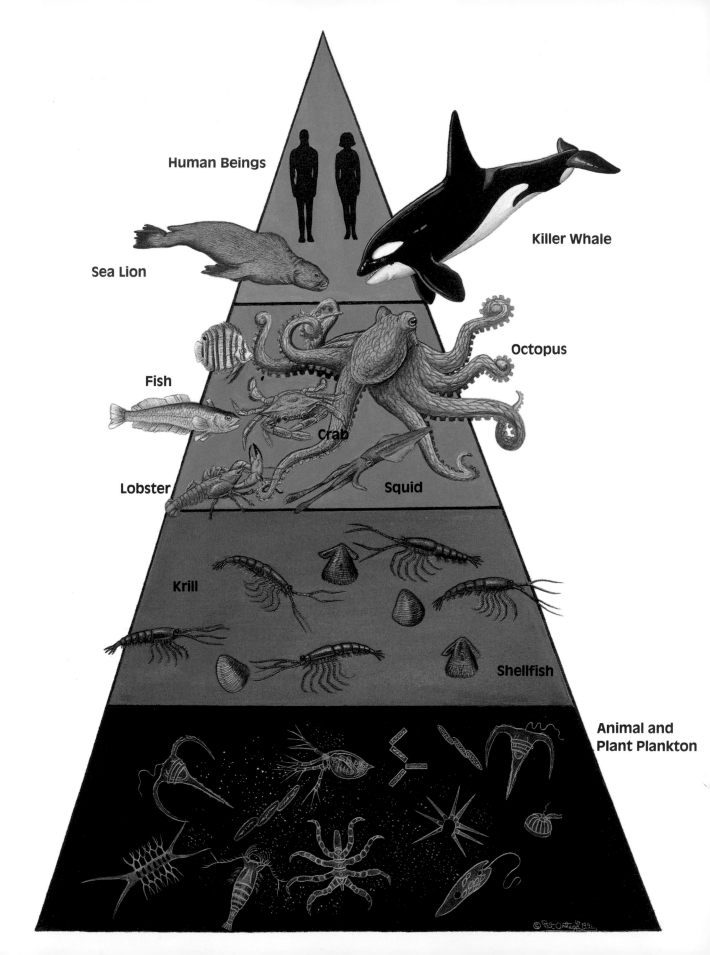

Respecting the Pyramid of Life

Ocean life can be arranged in a pyramid. Many of the creatures that live there depend on each other as sources of food. At the base of the pyramid are plankton, trillions of plants and animals so small you need a microscope to see them. Shellfish called copepods form the next layer of the pyramid. Copepods feed on plankton and are the main food for many larger animals.

In the middle of the pyramid are all the animals that feed on copepods, from tiny sardines to gigantic whales. At the top are the fish-eaters. These include humans and the really big fish, such as sharks. Marine mammals, such as seals and killer whales, are also at the top.

When we poison the oceans, we poison ourselves. Small amounts of pollutants seem harmless to plankton and other tiny ocean creatures. But they pass these pollutants on to the larger animals that feed on them. Many people have become sick or died from eating fish and shellfish raised in polluted areas. Scientists believe that eating some poisoned fish may even cause cancer.

Above: The peregrine falcon is dying out because it eats fish that have stored DDT, a deadly pesticide, in their bodies. DDT makes the falcon's egg-shells too thin. The eggs break before the chicks can hatch. In Britain, where DDT is banned, the peregrine falcon is making a comeback.

Opposite: A food chain is a network of animals, each kind dependent on another as food. Larger animals usually eat smaller ones. The ocean food chain begins with fish-eaters at the top, including humans and marine mammals. Next are fish and crustaceans, such as the crab and lobster. Krill and shellfish are next, followed by tiny plankton, which are the most plentiful ocean creatures.

Stopping Raw Sewage Dumping

Trashing the Beach

Beach trash can be deadly. Fish and marine mammals choke on plastic bags and six-pack rings. Medical wastes wash up on shore, carrying diseases. In the United States, three bottles of blood with the deadly AIDS virus were found on an East Coast beach.

Opposite, top: Sewage flows into the Mediterranean Sea.

Most communities dump human wastes, called sewage, into rivers, lakes, or oceans. Sewage does no harm if it is treated to remove deadly germs. But raw or untreated sewage can cause great environmental damage.

Untreated sewage causes disease. Swimmers in waters with high sewage levels become sick. Some people have died from eating shellfish and fish that lived in sewage-filled water. Sewage also acts as a **fertilizer**. It causes algae to grow out of control and kill marine plants. Sewage, along with other pollutants, lowers the oxygen levels in the water so that the fish die.

It is very expensive to build good sewage treatment plants, but some communities have done so. Scientists are working on ways to put sewage to good use. In Taiwan and the United States, treated sewage is used to enrich the waters of fish ponds. Some cities sell their treated sewage for fertilizer.

Opposite, bottom: When algae grows out of control, it uses up the oxygen that other forms of life need to grow.

Controlling Toxic Runoff from the Land

When it rains, tons of wastes wash off city streets and into rivers that flow into the sea. In coastal towns, pet wastes, lawn fertilizer, oil, and other pollutants wash right into the sea. In the country, pesticides, crop fertilizers, weed killers, and topsoil wash off farmers' fields and into rivers. Fertilizers cause some ocean plants to grow out of control and crowd out all others.

Opposite, upper: Clover plants, which usually have three-lobed leaves, help to build up soil nutrients — especially nitrogen.

Opposite, lower: This farm in Pennsylvania has been plowed according to the natural sloping patterns of the land. This method, called contour farming, helps conserve rainwater and reduce soil erosion.

Below: A Colorado farm shows how rain washes away topsoil into nearby rivers. Pesticides, weed killers, and fertilizers also wash off into the running water.

This toxic runoff is much harder to control than pollution from factories or sewage treatment plants. Still, some things have been done. Local governments in the state of Florida have passed laws to limit building near the shore. In many countries, the deadly pesticide DDT has been banned. Farmers prevent the loss of their topsoil by **contour plowing** or planting cover crops, such as clover, over bare fields. They also change the crops in their fields from one year to the next and so use fewer pesticides and weed killers.

Cooling the Hot-Water Pollution

You don't have to dump anything in the sea to pollute it. All you have to do is heat it up. **Nuclear power plants** and other industries sometimes use seawater to cool their machinery. When this heated water is flushed back into the sea, marine life suffers. For many fish, the warmer water temperature is a signal to lay eggs. The warmed water tricks the fish into laying eggs too early in the year. When this happens, their young can't find enough food and die.

Heated water doesn't have to be flushed back into the sea. In Sweden, hot water from a nuclear plant is used to warm an entire village in winter. And in the U.S., heated water from a factory in Oregon is sprayed into the air to water orchards.

Deadly Wastes of the Deep

Nuclear power plants also produce toxic wastes that last for thousands of years. These wastes cause cancer and other illnesses, yet the United States and some European countries have dumped them into the sea. Greenpeace, an environmental group, is working to stop nuclear dumping. Its members drive their boats right under the tipping platforms of waste ships. Other groups fight the building of new nuclear plants. In the U.S., few new plants are being built.

Opposite: The Dounreay Nuclear Power Plant in Scotland uses water from the nearby sea to cool its machinery.

Left: Heated water flows to the sea from a nuclear power plant.

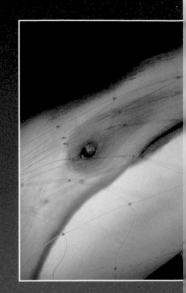

Dolphin-Safe Tuna

Tens of thousands of dolphins have drowned in nets used by tuna fishermen. Most large tuna companies now claim to use nets that allow dolphins to escape. A special "dolphin-safe" label on tuna cans tells shoppers which tuna was caught without harming dolphins.

Stopping Slaughter on the High Seas

Some types of fish are becoming scarce due to overfishing. This occurs when too many fish are caught and not enough are left to mate and lay eggs. In the North Sea, the herring have vanished because of overfishing.

Many nations are now working together to stop overfishing. For example, most countries in North America and Europe have signed an agreement to harvest only a limited number of salmon from the North Atlantic.

Fishing nets are another danger. They cause the accidental death of countless sea creatures. The worst damage has probably been caused by gill nets. These are fishing nets, and yet each year they snag at least 750,000 sea birds, 20,000 dolphins, 700 fur seals, and many small whales.

To stop this tragic slaughter, certain kinds of nets are no longer in use. Wide-mesh nets are banned in California because over 2,000 California sea otters have drowned in them.

Left: Fishing nets trap thousands of dolphins each year. Seals and even whales also get caught in these nets.

Inset: Air-breathing mammals, such as this dolphin, drown if they stay underwater too long.

25

Preserving Ocean Life

Opposite: The Great Barrier Reef off the coast of Australia is the largest underwater park in the world. The reef stretches for 995 miles (1,600 km)!

People around the world have banded together to save the oceans. Sometimes they form groups that work to preserve just one small area. In the state of New Jersey, for example, SOS — Save Our Shores — is a group that works against ocean dumping along the eastern coast of the United States. Other groups, such as Greenpeace, fight against worldwide ocean damage. They work to save whales and other marine mammals from extinction. They fight toxic ocean dumping, and they try to stop nuclear-bomb testing in the Pacific.

The oceans of the world belong to everybody — not to any one country. We must always be on guard against people who harm them. Together we must work to keep the oceans clean and safe for ourselves and for the animals that live in their waters.

Saving Coral Reefs

Some countries have set up underwater parks to protect parts of the ocean near their shores. Many of these parks contain fragile coral reefs, which are easily killed by pollution or toxic runoff, or damaged by divers and boat anchors. When coral reefs die, the marine life they shelter also disappears.

RESEARCH ACTIVITIES

1. **Build an aquarium.**
   Even if you live far from the sea, you can study
   sea life in your own home or classroom. You can
   find most of the materials you will need at a pet
   store: a fish tank, artificial salt mix, a filter
   system, a hydrometer to test the salt water, a
   thermometer and heater, and fish. You will also
   need tap water from the faucets at home.

2. Learn more about sharks.

Some sharks are fairly small, while others are huge. Some will eat humans, while others are harmless to them. Visit the library. Make a list of the different kinds of sharks, how big they are, and what they like to eat.

3. Find out more about nuclear power.

Make a list of the benefits of nuclear power and a list of its dangers. Compare the good and bad qualities of nuclear power with other energy sources, such as coal, hydroelectricity, and solar power.

Things You Can Do to Help

There are many things that you can do to help stop the pollution of the oceans and seas. The following activities will get you started. Try to involve your friends, family, and classmates in your conservation efforts, too.

1. **Recycle your garbage.** Help prevent the deaths of two million sea birds and 100,000 sea mammals each year that die from garbage dumped into the sea. Buy reusable products and things that come in recyclable containers. Recycle your plastic containers, glass bottles, and newspapers.

2. **Visit the grocery store.** Make a list of all the brands of tuna that have a dolphin-safe label and all the brands that don't. Post this list in your classroom. Tell your friends and classmates to buy only dolphin-safe tuna.

3. **Visit a sewage treatment plant.** Find out where your local sewage goes and what it does to your environment. Is the sewage treatment plant doing a good job? If not, get your friends and classmates to sign a petition asking for sewage treatment to be improved. Send the petition to the head of the plant, your mayor, or your department of natural resources.

Places to Write for More Information

The following organizations work to help save the oceans. When you write to them for more information, be specific about what you want to know.

Greenpeace USA
1436 U Street NW
Washington, D.C. 20009

Greenpeace (Canada)
2623 West 4th Avenue
Vancouver, British
    Columbia V6K 1P8

Sea Shepherd
    Conservation Society
P.O. Box 7000 S
Redondo Beach,
    California 90277

More Books to Read

Animals that Live in the Sea, by Joan Ann Straker (National Geographic Society)
The Mysterious Undersea World, by Jan Leslie Cook (National Geographic Society)
Seas and Oceans, by David Lambert (Facts on File)

Glossary

contour plowing — plowing along the natural dips and curves of the land

copepods — small shellfish similar to shrimp

current — a rapidly flowing stream of water within a surrounding body of water

extinction — the dying out of all members of a plant or animal species

fertilizer — a substance added to the soil to make plants grow better

mammal — any animal that receives milk from its mother's body

nuclear power plant — an electrical power plant that produces energy using dangerous nuclear fuels

oceans — great bodies of salt water that surround the continents

oxygen — one of the main gases that makes up the air we breathe

pesticides — poisons and chemicals used to kill insects

plankton — tiny plants and animals that drift in the sea

pollutants — poisonous substances that harm the air, water, or soil

sewage — human wastes carried through pipes by water

species — a group of animals or plants that share the same physical characteristics

tides — the regular rising and falling of the ocean's water level

toxic — poisonous

Index